CONTENT

PREFACE

Welcome to "In the Garden of Kindred Spirits" the second installment in the Mindful Adventures Trilogy, tailored for children aged 9 to 16. Within these pages, young readers are invited to embark on a journey that introduces them to the enchanting realms of mindfulness and nonduality.

This book goes beyond mere storytelling–it's an immersive experience designed to spark self-reflection, creativity, and an awareness of the profound interconnectedness that threads through every aspect of life. As we delve into this adventure together, we'll encourage artistic expression, emotional awareness, and an understanding of the intricate dance of emotions and relationships within the sanctuary of the mind.

The garden of your mind is a beautiful place, a place where seeds of mindfulness and nonduality are sown. Through the exploration of personal experiences and the symbolism of the breath of life, children will be guided to reflect on the unity that binds us all.

Guided meditations, like the one with Harmony in the meadow, will lead young minds on sensory journeys, exploring themes of fear, interconnectedness, and self-acceptance. Harmony's meadow becomes a playground for understanding the interconnected dance of life.

In the chapters that follow, children are encouraged to express their emotions, reflect on their unique qualities, and explore the connections that make their lives vibrant. Through this process, they will develop self-awareness and empathy, nurturing the seeds of compassion that will blossom as they navigate the rich landscape of their emotions and relationships.

So, young readers, as you turn the pages of this book, remember that your journey in the garden of your mind is an artistic expression, a canvas waiting for the strokes of your creativity. Every thought, every feeling, and every connection contributes to the masterpiece of your existence.

May this book be a companion on your journey of self-discovery, mindfulness, and understanding the beautiful tapestry of connections that make you a unique and integral part of the world.

~ Mohan Chute

ACKNOWLEDGMENTS

This book, "In the Garden of Kindred Spirits", is the result of a collective effort, nurtured by the kindness and generosity of many people. Their contributions are like vines reaching for the sun, spreading their beauty and fragrance throughout the stories.

I am deeply grateful to Shri Sharad Patil, a spiritual mentor and former Additional Collector of the Government of Maharashtra, IN. He has been more than a supporter, he has been a beacon of light in my journey, a close friend, and a fellow traveler. His steadfast belief in this project and constant motivation have been a powerful catalyst, enriching every step.

To all those who helped, directly or indirectly, my sincere appreciation. Your joint efforts have paved the way, allowing these stories to flourish in the hearts and minds of readers.

I express my heartfelt gratitude to my teachers, mentors, and contemporary sages, whose wisdom has been the sunlight that nourished my path. Your shared insights continue to guide me on this ongoing journey. And to every reader who explores this garden of awareness, may these stories be a gentle friend on your own quest for the essence of being.

Lastly, I express gratitude to the cutting-edge AI tools, including ChatGPT, Microsoft Copilot, and Google Bard, which served as invaluable collaborators in refining the content, polishing the prose, and ensuring proper spelling and grammar. Their assistance allowed me to delve into the deeper aspects of the stories, and for that, I am sincerely thankful. Recognition is also extended to RunwayML and DALL·E 3 for their role in generating AI-aided images.

It is a testament to our era that even Artificial Intelligence can contribute to this cosmic dance, helping us attune to the stillness and silence within. With their support, this garden has flourished into a space where technology and spirituality converge, serving as a reminder that we are all interconnected parts of the same cosmos.

May you find wonder and peace amidst these blossoms, dear reader.

~ Mohan Chute

One

The Garden of Harmony

The Curious Flower Lily and the Wise Old Bodhi Tree

Once upon a time, in a garden bursting with colors and sweet smells, lived a curious little flower named Lily. Unlike the other flowers content with their beauty, Lily couldn't stop wondering,

Who am I?

Am I just this delicate petal, this vibrant color, this sweet scent?

One sunny morning, Lily decided to seek the wisdom of Old Bodhi, a towering tree who had witnessed countless sunrises and moonlit nights.

"Oh, wise Bodhi," Lily whispered,

"who am I?"

Old Bodhi smiled gently, his branches swaying in the breeze.

"Little Lily, you are more than just a petal, a color, or a scent. You are part of this magnificent garden, a single thread in a tapestry of vibrant life."

Lily's petals twitched in surprise.

"But how can that be? I am so small and the garden is so vast!"

"Just like the waves are connected to the ocean, Lily," Old Bodhi explained, "each flower, tree, and even the butterflies fluttering by, share the same life force. We are all ripples in the same vast pond of existence."

Lily's heart swelled with joy. She closed her eyes and felt a connection to everything around her. The gentle hum of the bees, the soft rustle of leaves, the warm sun on her petals - they were all part of her, and she was part of them.

From that day on, Lily looked at the garden with new eyes. She saw not just her own beauty, but the beauty of everything around her. She learned to appreciate the diversity of colors, shapes, and scents, knowing that they all contributed to the magic of the garden.

And so, little Lily, the once curious flower, blossomed into a symbol of awareness and unity, reminding everyone in the garden that true beauty lies in recognizing the interconnectedness of all things.

1.1 Guided Meditation

- Find a comfortable spot, sitting or lying down, and close your eyes. Take a deep breath in, filling your lungs with air. Imagine you are in a magical garden, filled with colorful flowers, each representing a unique part of you.

- Picture yourself as a flower, just like Lily in our story. Feel the warmth of the sun on your petals, the gentle breeze caressing your leaves, and the soft ground beneath your roots. As you breathe in, imagine drawing in the energy of the entire garden. Feel the connection with every flower, tree, and butterfly fluttering by. You are part of this vibrant tapestry of life.

- With each breath out, release any worries or doubts that you may have. Allow yourself to relax, knowing that, just like the flowers in the garden, you have a special place in the world.

- In the center of the garden, visualize the wise old tree, Bodhi. Imagine its branches reaching out, connecting with every living thing. Sense the wisdom it shares, reassuring you that you are an essential part of this beautiful garden.

- With each breath, watch the colors around you become brighter, the fragrances more enchanting. You are not just a petal; you are an integral part of the harmonious dance of life.

- Take a moment to appreciate the interconnectedness of all things. Each flower, each tree, and every butterfly contributes to the garden's vibrant story. Embrace this feeling of oneness.

- Slowly wiggle your fingers and toes, take a few deep breaths, and when you are ready, gently open your eyes, carrying this feeling of harmony with you. Remember, like the flowers in the garden, you are unique and valuable, contributing to the beauty of the world.

To access additional meditations and resources, scan the QR code

1.2 (A) Worksheet

(A) Draw Your Flower

Create your unique flower by drawing its petals. Each petal can represent a different aspect of yourself—your interests, talents, or favorite things.

1.2 (B) Worksheet

(B) Write a Garden Poem

Express your feelings about being part of the interconnected garden. Write a short poem celebrating the beauty of diversity and oneness.

Two
Harmony's Melody
The Stream's Tale of Connection

In a magical garden filled with vibrant flowers, a playful stream named Sparkle gurgled and danced through its heart. Sparkle was the garden's lifeblood, its rippling waters whispering secrets to the flowers as they swayed in the gentle breeze.

One day, Sparkle asked the flowers, "Dear friends, have you ever noticed that though we appear different, our roots all reach down to my cool water and share the same nourishing earth?"

The flowers, curious and intrigued, leaned closer to listen. Sparkle continued, "When the rain falls from the sky, I carry its gifts to each of you, nourishing your roots and helping you grow tall and strong.

Though you may seem separate, you are all connected through my water and the earth. Just like the branches of a majestic tree, you each have your unique beauty and fragrance, yet your essence is shared."

As Sparkle spoke, the flowers gasped with realization. They understood that their very existence depended on the same life-giving water and the fertile soil. They were not simply individual flowers, but a vibrant community interconnected through the gentle flow of Sparkle. And Sparkle itself was not just a stream, but a vital thread woven into the tapestry of the entire garden.

This story reminds us that even though things may seem separate on the surface, there's an invisible thread that connects us all. We are like different instruments in a grand orchestra, each playing our own unique notes, yet contributing to the beautiful symphony of life. Just like Sparkle and the flowers, we are all part of something much bigger and more wonderful than ourselves.

2.1 Guided Meditation

- Find a quiet and comfortable space to sit or lie down. Take a deep breath in and imagine yourself in the magical garden beside the gentle stream.

- Close your eyes and picture the flowing water of the stream. Sense the soothing sound it makes as it travels through the garden, connecting everything in its path.

- Imagine yourself as one of the flowers by the stream. Feel the coolness of the water, and let it symbolize the interconnectedness of all living things, just like the stream connects the garden.

- Take a deep breath, inhaling the freshness of the air around the stream. As you exhale, release any tension or worries, letting them flow away with the stream.

- Envision the roots of your flower reaching down into the earth, touching the same soil as the other flowers. Sense the shared foundation that connects you all.

- Picture the rain starting to fall, nourishing the soil and feeding the stream. Feel the water moving through your roots, connecting you with every other flower in the garden.

- With each breath, visualize the stream carrying away any negative thoughts or feelings, leaving you with a sense of calm and connection.

- Imagine the sun shining above, casting a warm glow on the garden. Feel the energy of the sun infusing every part of the garden, including you.

- Open your heart to the idea that, just like the flowers and the stream, you are part of a beautiful symphony of life. Each note is unique, contributing to the melody of harmony.

- Slowly open your eyes, bringing this sense of interconnected harmony with you into the world. Remember that, like the flowers by the stream, you are connected to the greater flow of life.

To access additional meditations and resources, scan the QR code

2.2 (A) Worksheet 

(A) Draw Your Flower by the Stream:

Illustrate yourself as a flower by the stream. Include details like the water, soil, and sunlight. Be creative with colors and shapes.

2.2 (B) Worksheet

(B) Sun of Positivity

The sun above the garden, symbolizing positivity and warmth. Write down positive affirmations or things that make you happy around the sun.

 # 2.2 (C-D) Worksheet

(C) Stream of Emotions

On a separate sheet draw a representation of your emotions flowing like the stream. Use different colors to express various feelings. Reflect on how your emotions, just like the stream, are a natural part of life.

(D) Harmony Collage

On a separate sheet cut out pictures from magazines or draw images that represent harmony to you. Create a collage that showcases the interconnectedness of different elements in nature.

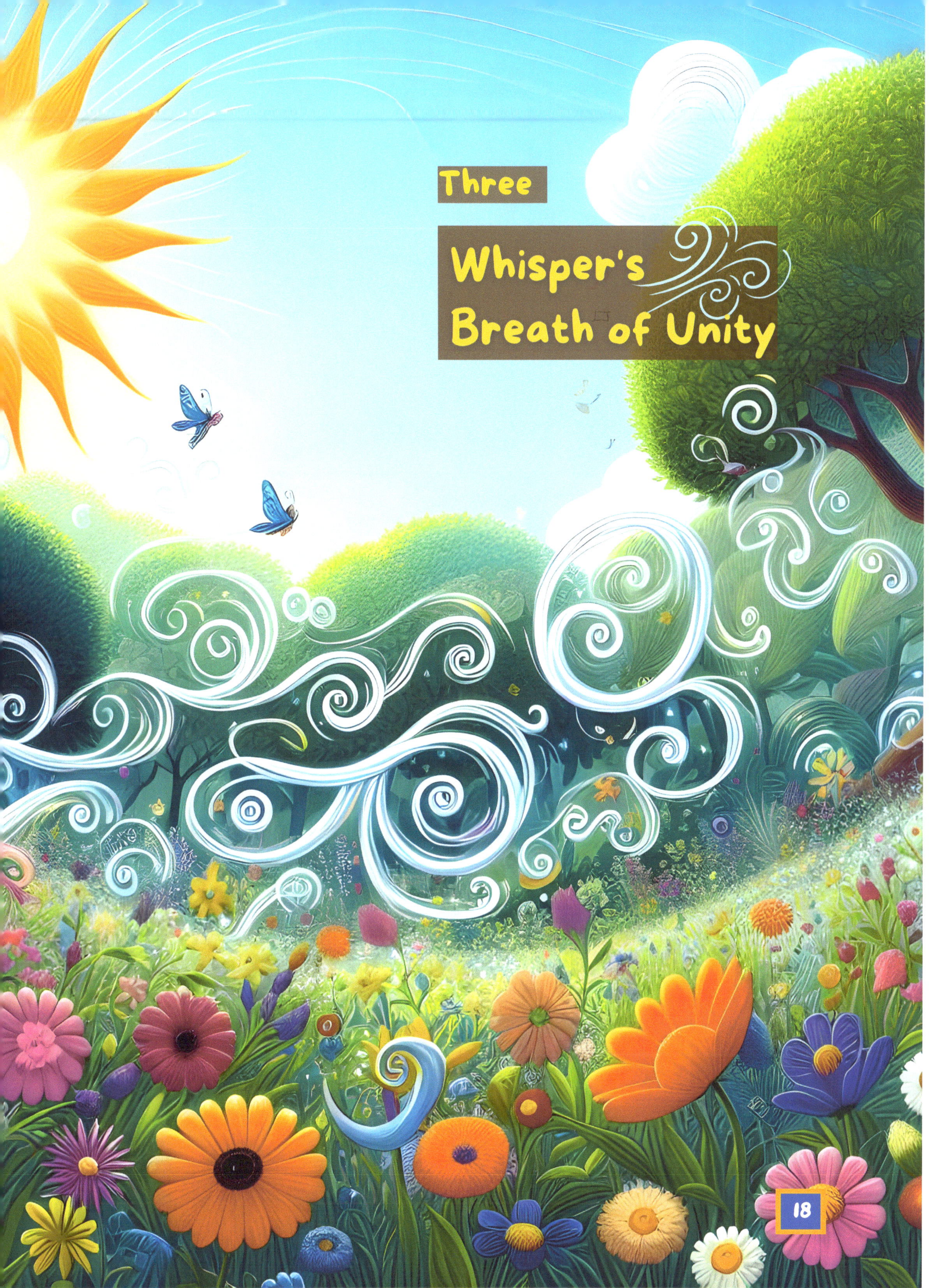
Three
Whisper's
Breath of Unity
18

One sunny morning, a playful breeze named Whisper danced through the magical garden. As it swirled around the colorful flowers and towering trees, it whispered a secret message, "Dear friends, have you ever considered the very air you breathe? This air, this breath of life, connects each and every one of us."

Intrigued by Whisper's words, the flowers swayed and the trees rustled. Whisper continued, "Just like the air that fills your lungs and gives you life, it connects every living being in this garden. It shows no favoritism, embracing all equally, big and small, tall and short."

As Whisper swirled and twirled, the flowers and trees felt a surge of unity. They realized that the air caressing one petal was the same air kissing another leaf, the same air whispering through every creature in the garden. It was a powerful reminder that the very essence of life, the breath itself, connects all living things.

This story teaches us that even though we may look different or have different roles in the garden, we are all connected by the invisible thread of air. We are all part of the same tapestry of life, sharing the same breath, the same source of existence. Just like Whisper, the air embraces all equally, reminding us that we are not alone, but part of something much bigger and more wonderful than ourselves.

3.1 Guided Meditation

- Find a comfortable space where you can sit or lie down. Take a few deep breaths to settle into a relaxed state.
- Close your eyes and imagine yourself in the magical garden filled with colorful flowers and towering trees. Feel the warmth of the sun on your face.
- Picture a gentle breeze named Whisper entering the scene. As you breathe in, imagine that you are inhaling the same playful breeze that connects all living things in the garden.
- With each inhale, visualize the air filling your lungs and bringing a sense of unity. Feel the connection between your breath and the breath of the flowers, trees, and all the creatures around you.
- As you exhale, release any tension or worries. Picture your breath swirling and dancing like Whisper, creating a harmonious flow of energy.
- Imagine the flowers and trees swaying in response to the shared breath, acknowledging the interconnectedness that binds them together.
- Visualize the invisible thread of air linking each living being in the garden. See it weaving a tapestry of unity, connecting everyone in a dance of life.
- Take a moment to appreciate the diversity in the garden. Each flower and tree is unique, yet they all share the same breath, the same source of life.
- Feel a sense of oneness with the garden and all its inhabitants. Sense the invisible bond created by the simple act of breathing.
- Slowly open your eyes, bringing the awareness of connection and unity with you. Carry this feeling throughout your day, knowing that, like Whisper's breath, you are part of a beautiful dance of life.

To access additional meditations and resources, scan the QR code

3.2 (A) Worksheet

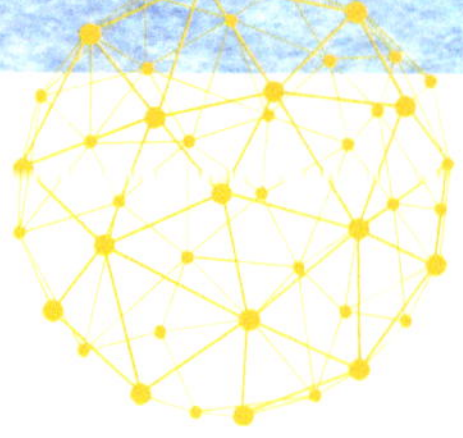

(A) Invisible Threads:

Draw invisible threads connecting different elements in your garden.
Write down qualities or things that connect these elements, just like the invisible thread of air.

3.2 (B) Worksheet

(B) Breath of Unity:

Draw or write about a moment when you felt a sense of unity or connection with others. It could be during a family gathering, playing with friends, or any shared experience.

3.2 (C) Worksheet

(C) Unity Affirmations

Write down affirmations or positive statements about unity and connection. Place them around your garden scene to remind yourself of the invisible threads that bind us all.

Four
The Whispers of the Thoughtful Garden
24

In the heart of a magical garden, where the leaves rustled and flowers bloomed, there hid a special place. It was a secret haven where thoughts, like colorful wildflowers, unfolded in all sorts of colors and shapes. Each thought had its own melody, creating a magical symphony.

Kids, full of curiosity, often found this hidden spot. The garden welcomed them, and the flowers kindly invited them to be part of a grand show. "Close your eyes, little ones," the flowers rustled, dancing in a rhythm. "Listen to the magical tunes of your thoughts."
As the kids closed their eyes, something amazing happened. The world around them disappeared, and a mix of sights and sounds filled their minds.

Thoughts fluttered like butterflies, creating lively pictures. Some thoughts danced like playful puppies, while others glided gracefully, like a swan. Each had its special melody, a unique note in the ever-changing symphony.

The flowers, with soft voices, shared wise words with the children. "Just as our garden has different flowers, your mind has a variety of thoughts," they explained. "Cherish them, little ones, for they make you who you are. They add color to your world, shape your dreams, and guide you on your journey of discovering yourself."

Listening to the flowers, the children learned to see the beauty in their own minds. They discovered how to watch their thoughts not with judgment but with wonder. Every little thought, no matter how quick, became a part of the beautiful melody of their being.

From that special day, the children carried the garden's wisdom in their hearts. They knew their thoughts weren't just tools but living parts, each contributing to the unique melody of their lives. So, with joy and gratitude, they continued exploring the vast garden of their minds, embracing the magical symphony of their thoughts.

4.1 Guided Meditation

Find a comfortable spot to sit or lie down, like a cozy corner in your room. Take a few deep breaths, letting go of any tension. Imagine yourself in a magical garden filled with colorful flowers and gentle whispers.

1. **Entering the Garden:** Close your eyes and envision the entrance to this enchanting garden. Picture the vibrant colors, the scent of blooming flowers, and the soft rustle of leaves.

2. **Meeting Your Thoughts:** As you explore the garden, notice a clearing where thoughts bloom like wildflowers. Imagine each thought as a unique flower, each with its own color and shape. Walk among them, feeling the soft grass beneath your feet.

3. **The Symphony Begins:** Now, sit or lie down in the middle of the clearing. Take a deep breath and listen. The flowers start to dance, and each thought creates its melody. Picture the thoughts swirling like butterflies, each contributing to the beautiful symphony of your mind.

4. **Observing Without Judgment:** Let the thoughts come and go. Observe them with curiosity, like watching a captivating performance. If a thought is like a playful puppy or a graceful swan, simply notice without judgment.

5. **Words of Wisdom from the Flowers:** Imagine the flowers speaking softly, sharing wisdom about the diversity of your thoughts. Embrace them, for they are the essence of who you are. Let their words guide you on a journey of self-discovery.

6. **Gratitude and Joy:** As the symphony continues, feel gratitude for the variety of thoughts in your mind. Each one is a unique note, shaping the melody of your life. Embrace the joy of this beautiful symphony.

7. **Returning to the Present:** Slowly become aware of your surroundings. Open your eyes and take a moment to appreciate the symphony of your thoughts. Carry the peace and wisdom of the garden with you.

To access additional meditations and resources, scan the QR code

4.2 (A) Worksheet

(A) Draw Your Garden:

Use colors and shapes to draw the magical garden from the meditation.
Include the flowers representing your thoughts.
What colors do you see?
How do the flowers dance?

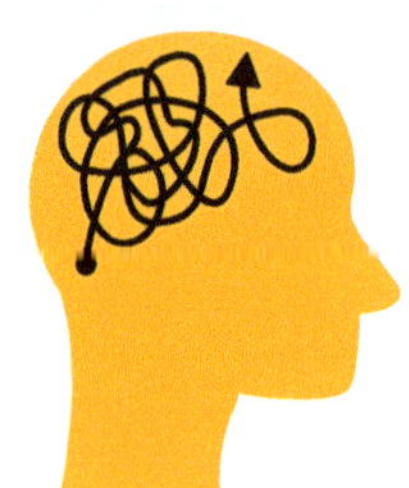

4.2 (B) Worksheet

(B) Name Your Thoughts

Write down different thoughts you often have. Give each thought a name based on its "personality" or how it feels. For example, "Joyful Jester" for happy thoughts or "Curious Explorer" for inquisitive thoughts.

(C) Create a Thought Symphony:

Create a Thought Symphony: Imagine your thoughts as music notes. Draw musical symbols (like notes and clefs) beside each thought.
What kind of music would your thoughts create together?
Draw the musical instruments your thoughts might resemble.

4.2 (D) Worksheet

(D) Reflection

- Write a short paragraph reflecting on the diversity of your thoughts.
  How do they contribute to the unique symphony of your mind?
  What did you learn from observing them without judgment?

Five
The Magical Painting in the Garden

In a secret part of the garden, where sunlight played hide-and-seek through the leaves, there stood an extraordinary canvas. This wasn't just any ordinary canvas; it shimmered with an otherworldly luminescence, its surface constantly shifting and changing, reflecting the myriad perceptions of those who gazed upon it.

Next to the canvas was a very old tree called Bodhi. Its branches reached up high like old fingers, and it loved telling stories about many seasons. Its leaves, full of smartness, whispered gently in the wind, calling the kids closer. "Come, little friends," creaked the Bodhi tree,

sounding like a mix of the wind and leaves. "Look at the canvas and tell me, what do you see?"

The kids, excited about the magical painting and curious about the old tree's words, came closer. Each one expected to see the same thing, but when they stared, they saw different amazing pictures.

One child saw a busy city with lots of people and tall buildings. Another saw a calm field, all lit up by the morning sun and covered in flowers with morning dew. One more saw a wild seashore, where waves crashed loudly against the land.

The Bodhi tree chuckled, its branches moving with joy. "Your way of seeing things," it explained, "is like an artist's brush. Each of you paints a special picture on the canvas of your world. Every brush is different, shaped by what you've been through, your feelings, and what you believe. There's no one 'right' picture because the real beauty is in the many ways you see things."

The kids, amazed by the Bodhi tree's wise words, started seeing the world in a new way. They understood that how they saw things, from their own adventures, made their own worlds. They learned to respect how others saw things, knowing that each painting on the canvas of reality made the world more interesting.

From that day on, the kids kept this new understanding in their hearts. They looked at the world with wide eyes and open minds, celebrating the beauty of differences and knowing that everyone's way of seeing things was special. They discovered that the real magic wasn't in finding one "true" picture but in enjoying the always-changing painting of reality, created by everyone's unique brushes.

5.1 Guided Meditation

The Magical Painting in the Garden

- Close your eyes and imagine yourself in a magical garden. Picture a beautiful canvas standing in a hidden corner, glowing with a special light. This canvas is yours to paint, and it's always changing, just like the canvas in the story.

- Take a deep breath in and slowly exhale. As you breathe, feel the warm sunlight on your face and hear the gentle rustling of leaves in the wind. Now, approach the enchanted canvas.

- With each breath, think about the unique picture you want to paint on the canvas. Imagine the colors, shapes, and scenes that represent your thoughts and feelings. Let your imagination run wild, just like the kids in the story.

- As you paint on the canvas of your mind, notice the magical glow intensifying. Your thoughts are creating a masterpiece, and it's entirely your own. Embrace the beauty of your perceptions and let the canvas shift and change with every stroke.

- Now, listen to the wise Bodhi tree nearby. Hear its soothing voice telling you that there's no right or wrong painting—only the beauty in the diversity of your thoughts. Feel the connection between your inner canvas and the canvas in the garden.

- Take a moment to appreciate the uniqueness of your painting and the paintings of others. Open your eyes, carrying the enchantment of the canvas into your day.

To access additional meditations and resources, scan the QR code

5.2 (A) Worksheet

(A) Draw your enchanted canvas:

What colors and scenes represent your thoughts and feelings today?

5.2 (B) Worksheet

(B) Description of your canvas

Write a short description of your canvas. What makes your painting special and unique to you?

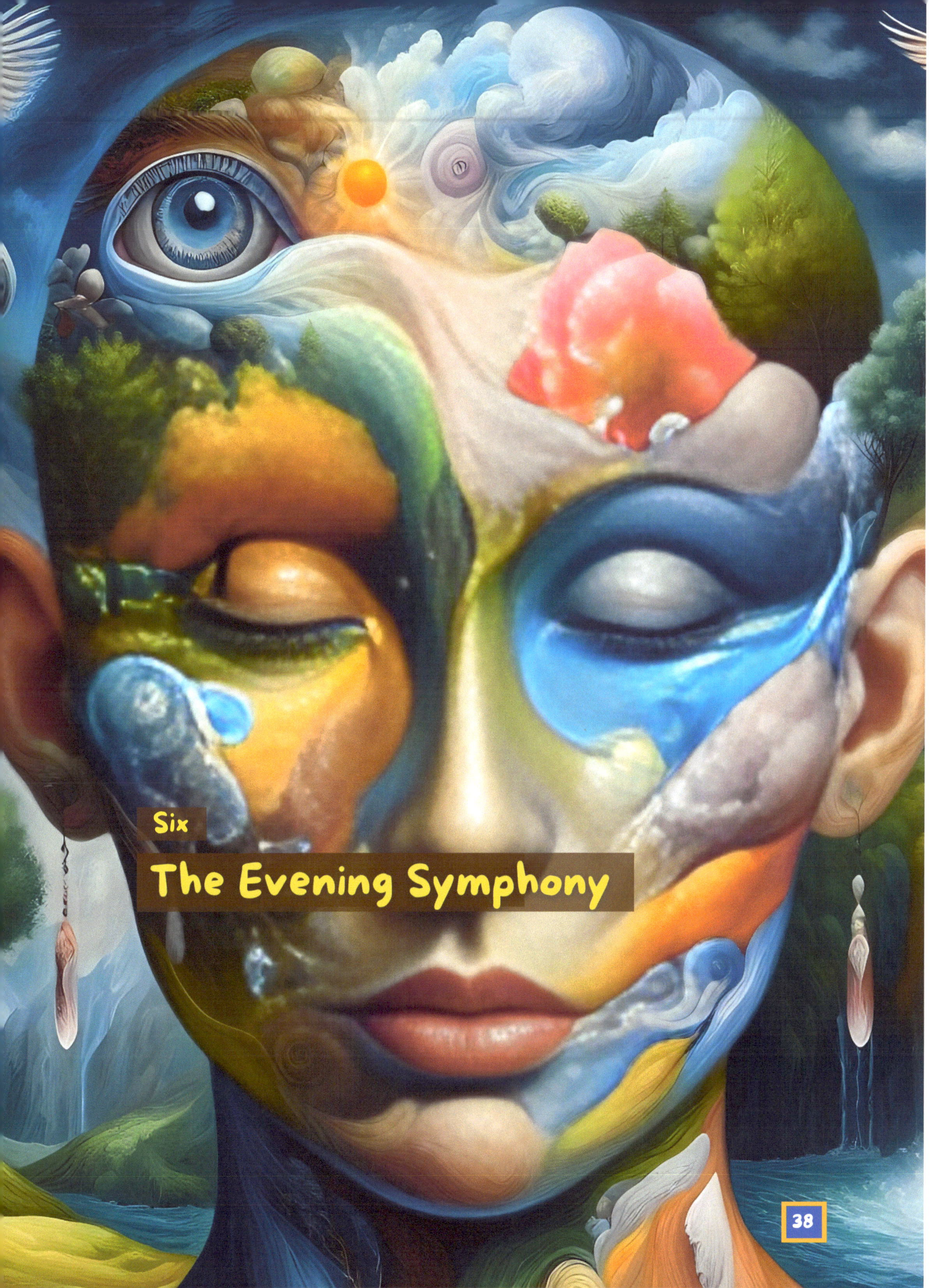
Six
The Evening Symphony

As the sun set and shadows stretched across the garden, something magical unfolded. A beautiful dance of senses began, creating a colorful experience for the children. Each sense took its turn, guiding the kids on a special journey.

First, Sight painted the world with vibrant colors. The sky turned into a stunning canvas of red, gold, and indigo. The ancient trees' leaves shimmered in the fading light, outlined in a soft glow.

Then, Sound filled the air with a mesmerizing melody. Rustling leaves and chirping crickets became the orchestra, guided by the playful wind. The children closed their eyes, letting the rhythm of the world beat in their hearts. Touch came next, inviting the kids to feel the textures around them. They touched the cool grass, the rough tree bark, and felt the breeze on their faces. Each touch connected them to the present moment.

Taste stepped forward, offering the sweet nectar of evening dew and the freshness of the air. With closed eyes, the children savored the flavors, each taste adding a unique note to the symphony of life. Lastly, Smell took the stage, bringing fragrances of earth and wildflowers.

Inhaling deeply, the kids felt a rush of emotions and memories tied to each scent. The senses danced together, showing the children how everything was connected. Each sense played a part in their rich experience, like brushstrokes on a canvas. They realized that seeing, hearing, feeling, tasting, and smelling weren't separate but a harmonious symphony.

This magical dance under the twilight sky sparked wonder and curiosity in the children. They became active participants in life's grand choreography, appreciating the unique melody of their minds and the vibrant symphony of their senses.

From that day on, the children carried this awareness with them, embracing the world with open hearts and minds, ready to be enchanted by the ever-changing dance of their senses.

6.1 Guided Meditation

The Evening Symphony

1. Introduction: Find a comfortable, quiet space. Close your eyes and take a few deep breaths to relax.

2. Sight: Imagine a beautiful sunset, painting the sky with warm colors. Picture leaves shimmering in fading light. Notice the details, creating a vivid image in your mind.

3. Sound: Listen to the rustling leaves and chirping crickets. Feel the wind playing a melody, sending shivers of delight. With your closed eyes, immerse yourself in the soothing sounds.

4. Touch: Imagine walking barefoot on cool grass. Feel the rough bark of trees against your fingertips. Sense the gentle caress of the breeze on your face.

5. Taste: Picture tasting the sweet nectar of evening dew. Feel the freshness of the air as you breathe. Savour these flavors, each a unique note in the symphony.

6. Smell: Inhale deeply, sensing the fragrant aroma of the earth. Imagine the sweet scent of wildflowers filling the air. Let each smell evoke emotions and memories.

7. Symphony Unite: Envision all your senses working together, harmoniously. See the interconnected dance of your perceptions. Feel the symphony of your senses playing in unity.

8. Closing: Take a few moments to breathe deeply. When you're ready, gently open your eyes.

To access additional meditations and resources, scan the QR code

6.2 (A) Worksheet

(A) Sound Mapping:

Draw a map representing the sounds in the garden.
Connect lines to show how different sounds are linked.

(B)Texture Exploration:

Use words or drawings to describe how different textures feel.
Think about the cool grass, rough bark, and gentle breeze.

6.2 (C) Worksheet

(C) Flavorful Creations:

Design your own imaginary flavors inspired by the story.
What would the sweet nectar or fresh air taste like?

6.2 (D) Worksheet

(D) Scent Journey:

Create a list of scents that evoke memories or emotions.
Draw or write about each scent and its significance.

6.2 (E) Worksheet

(E) Symphony Visualization:

Draw or write about how you visualize your senses working together.
What does the symphony of your senses look like?

Seven
The Seed of Harmony
A Story of Courage and Connection
47

Deep within the heart of a vibrant meadow, nestled amongst the swaying grasses and wildflowers, lived a tiny seed named Harmony. Unlike the other seeds, filled with the unbridled enthusiasm of growth, Harmony was plagued by a persistent fear. It dreamt of blossoming into a magnificent flower, its petals shimmering with vibrant colors, but doubt gnawed at its core.

One bright morning, as the sun cast its warm glow across the meadow, a wise whisper danced on the breeze. It was the Wind, an ancient spirit who had observed the cycles of life for countless seasons.
Sensing Harmony's anxieties, the Wind approached the tiny seed.
"Little one," the Wind rustled gently, "why do you carry such a heavy heart?"

Harmony, hesitant but drawn to the Wind's soothing voice, confided in it. "I fear I won't grow to be as beautiful as the other flowers," it whispered sadly. "Their colors are so bold, their shapes so perfect, and their fragrances so enchanting. I fear my own bloom will be insignificant and unnoticed."

The Wind listened patiently, its whispers weaving a tapestry of understanding. "Little Harmony," it spoke, "the dance of nature is not a competition for grandeur. Each flower, no matter how small or

seemingly insignificant, contributes to the breathtaking beauty of this meadow. The delicate violets, the vibrant sunflowers, the fragrant lilies – they all play a unique role in creating this symphony of life."
The Wind paused, allowing its words to settle within Harmony's core.

"Understand, little one, that your fear arises from an illusion, a feeling of separateness. You are not an individual entity struggling alone. You are an integral part of this entire meadow, connected to every blade of grass and every flower by the invisible threads of life. Embrace your uniqueness, Harmony, for it is your very essence that adds to the richness and diversity of this vibrant tapestry."

As the Wind's words echoed through Harmony's being, a sense of calm washed over it. It began to see the meadow not as a collection of separate entities, but as a single, interconnected whole. The fear that had held it back began to melt away, replaced by a newfound sense of belonging and purpose. And so, Harmony grew. It pushed its roots deep into the fertile soil, drawing strength from the earth. It embraced the sun's warmth and the gentle rain, allowing them to nourish its growth. Slowly, steadily, it unfolded its petals, revealing a delicate bloom unlike any other.

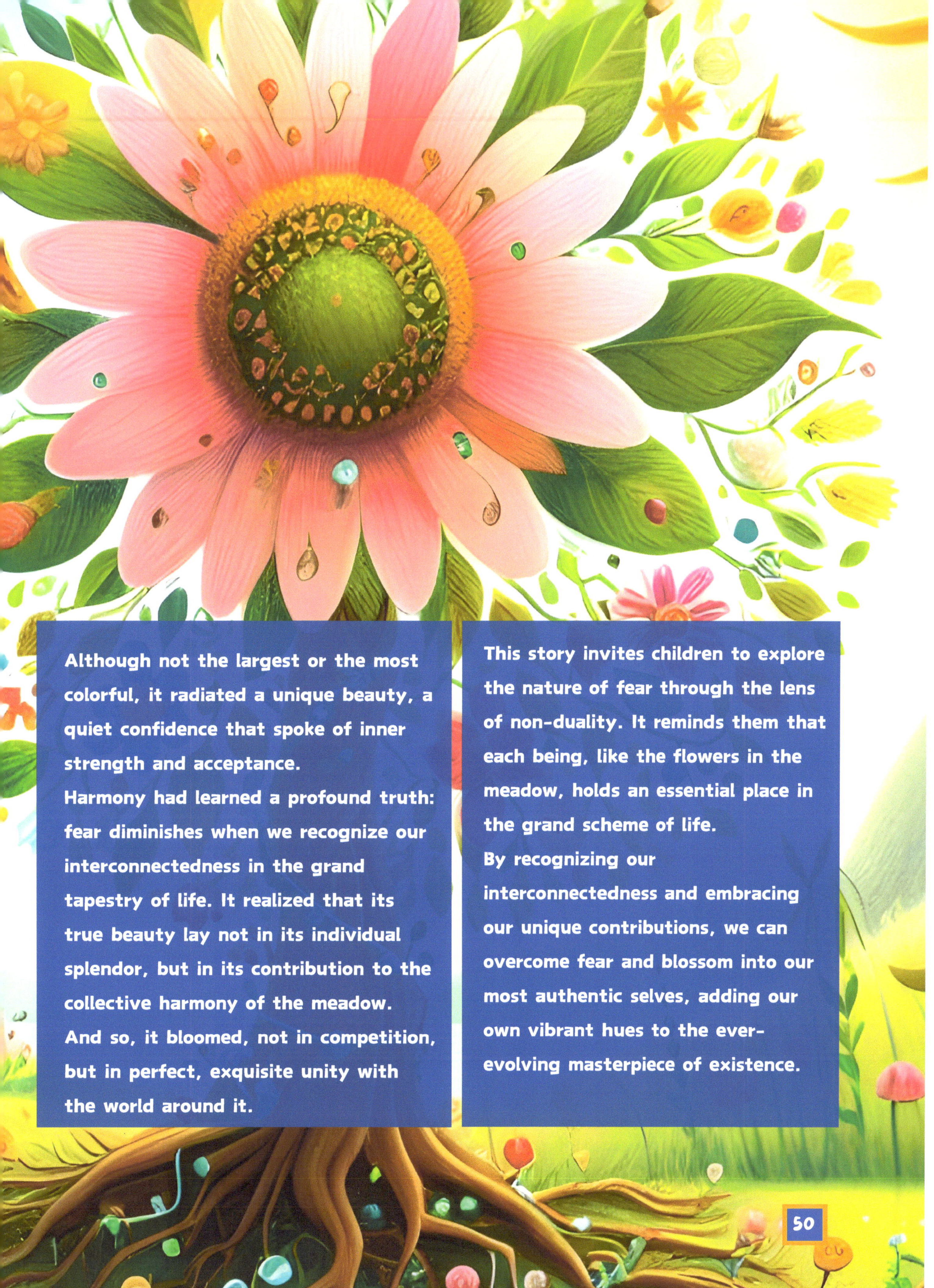

Although not the largest or the most colorful, it radiated a unique beauty, a quiet confidence that spoke of inner strength and acceptance.

Harmony had learned a profound truth: fear diminishes when we recognize our interconnectedness in the grand tapestry of life. It realized that its true beauty lay not in its individual splendor, but in its contribution to the collective harmony of the meadow.

And so, it bloomed, not in competition, but in perfect, exquisite unity with the world around it.

This story invites children to explore the nature of fear through the lens of non-duality. It reminds them that each being, like the flowers in the meadow, holds an essential place in the grand scheme of life.

By recognizing our interconnectedness and embracing our unique contributions, we can overcome fear and blossom into our most authentic selves, adding our own vibrant hues to the ever-evolving masterpiece of existence.

7.1 Guided Meditation

1. **Set the Scene:** Find a comfortable, quiet space to sit or lie down. Take a few deep breaths, letting go of tension.

2. **Immersing in the Meadow:** Close your eyes and imagine yourself in a vibrant meadow. Feel the softness of the grass beneath you and the warmth of the sun above.

3. **Meeting Harmony:** Picture a tiny seed named Harmony in the meadow. Sense its hesitations and fears about growing.

4. **Encounter with the Wind:** Envision the ancient Wind, a gentle spirit, approaching Harmony. Feel the soothing rustle of the Wind's whispers.

5. **Sharing Fears:** Imagine Harmony confiding in the Wind about its fears. Connect with the vulnerability and honesty in expressing fears.

6. **Wisdom of the Wind:** Listen to the Wind's words about interconnectedness. Feel the idea of being an integral part of a vast, interconnected meadow.

7. **Transformation of Harmony:** Sense Harmony's transformation as it absorbs the Wind's wisdom. Feel the fear melting away and a calm sense of belonging emerging.

8. **Growth and Unfolding:** Picture Harmony growing, roots sinking into fertile soil. Experience the unfolding of its petals, revealing a unique bloom.

9. **Understanding True Beauty:** Reflect on the profound truth Harmony learned. Recognize the beauty in interconnectedness and acceptance.

10. **Blossoming in Unity:** Envision Harmony blooming in perfect unity with the meadow. Feel the collective harmony of the meadow as each flower contributes.

11. **Closing:** Take a few moments to breathe deeply. When ready, gently open your eyes.

This guided meditation helps children explore the themes of fear, interconnectedness, and self-acceptance through a visual and sensory journey in the meadow with Harmony.

To access additional meditations and resources, scan the QR code

7.2 (A) Worksheet

(A) Draw Your Meadow and Express Your Emotions:

Sketch a meadow and include elements like grass, flowers, and the sun.
Use colors and symbols to represent emotions related to fear and belonging.

7.2 (B) Worksheet

(B) Create Your Bloom:

Draw a flower representing yourself, embracing your uniqueness.
Consider what makes your bloom special.

7.2 (C) Worksheet

(C) Connect with Others:

Write about how you feel connected to others.
What threads of connection do you see in your life?

Eight
Bodhi's Insight: A Symphony of Joy, Sorrow, and Healing

In a calm forest where sunlight peeked through the leaves and wise old trees whispered stories in the breeze, there stood a special tree called Bodhi. This tree had seen many happy and sad moments in the forest.

One day, a young deer named Grace, who had a little hurt on her leg, went to Bodhi. Her eyes were teary, and she wondered why there had to be pain in the beautiful forest.

Bodhi, with its branches reaching out like friendly arms, spoke gently to Grace. "Dear one, pain is like a special part of the dance of life in the forest.

Just as rain and sunshine help the forest grow, joy and pain are both important in the big dance of existence."
Grace, looking curious, asked, "But how can pain be part of the dance?"

Bodhi, swaying its branches like in a dance, explained, "Think of a beautiful melody, like a song. It has high and low notes, and each note is important. Life's melody is made of joy and sorrow, laughter and tears. Pain, even though it seems different, is like an important note that reminds us of how our body and mind are connected."

Grace's eyes lit up with understanding. "So, pain is not a punishment but a message?" she asked softly.

Bodhi nodded, its leaves making a soft sound. "Exactly," it whispered. "When pain comes, it's like a message telling us to listen to our bodies and minds. It's a sign to take a break, think, and start the healing process."

Closing her eyes, Grace felt calm. She realized that pain wasn't something to be scared of but a natural part of life's dance.

Bodhi had taught her that noticing pain, just like hearing all the different notes in a song, allows the healing music to play.

Since that day, Grace kept this understanding in her heart. She learned to welcome both happy and sad moments, knowing they were all part of life's beautiful dance. With this wisdom, she danced through the forest, feeling connected to the ever-changing rhythm of life.

8.1 Guided Meditation

Bodhi's Insight: A Symphony of Joy, Sorrow, and Healing

1. Begin by finding a quiet and comfortable space. Sit or lie down in a relaxed position.

2. Close your eyes and take a few deep breaths. Inhale slowly, feeling your chest and belly expand, and exhale gently, releasing any tension.

3. Imagine yourself in a serene forest, surrounded by tall trees and dappled sunlight. Picture the wise Bodhi tree standing nearby, its branches swaying gently in the breeze.

4. Focus on your breath, letting it become a soothing rhythm. Feel the forest air entering your lungs, bringing a sense of calm and peace.

5. In your mind's eye, visualize any worries or tensions as leaves on a tree. With each exhale, imagine these leaves gently falling away, carried by the breeze.

6. Now, envision a soft melody playing in the background, representing the dance of life. Picture both joyful and challenging moments as different notes in this harmonious melody.

7. As you breathe, acknowledge the various sensations in your body. If there's any discomfort or pain, see it as a note in the melody, a natural part of your unique rhythm.

8. Allow the melody to guide you through moments of joy and moments of healing. Embrace the completeness of the song, knowing that each note contributes to the beauty of your experience.

9. Focus on the idea that, like the forest's dance, your feelings and experiences are interconnected. Accept them as part of your journey.

10. When you're ready, gently bring your awareness back to the present moment. Open your eyes, and carry the sense of harmony with you.

To access additional meditations and resources, scan the QR code

8.2 (A) Worksheet

(A) Feelings Melody:

Draw a musical staff across your paper. In each note, write or draw a feeling you've experienced–joy, sadness, excitement, or calmness. Connect the notes with lines to show how they create a melody.

8.2 (B) Worksheet

(B) Message from Pain:

In a thought bubble near the deer, write or draw a message that pain might convey. It could be a reminder to listen to your body or take a break. Reflect on how pain can be a messenger.

8.2 (C) Worksheet

(C) My Healing Dance:

Draw yourself dancing in the forest. Represent your healing process by adding symbols like bandages turning into colorful ribbons or a sun symbolizing a new day.

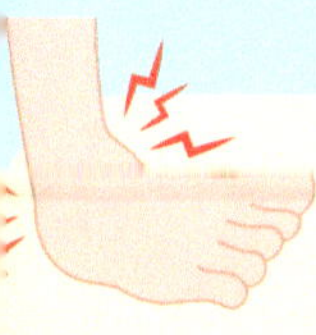

(D) Reflection:

Write a short paragraph reflecting on what you've learned from the guided meditation and the activity. How does understanding pain as a part of life's dance contribute to your sense of harmony?

Nine
The Forest Awakens
A Dance of Awareness

Deep within a magical forest, where the sun dappled the leaves with golden light, stood Bodhi, a wise old tree. Its roots anchored it deep in the earth, while its branches stretched towards the sky, reaching for the secrets whispered by the wind. This gentle giant was more than just a tree; it was the silent witness to a symphony of life, a dance of thoughts, feelings, and sensations unfolding before its ancient eyes.

One day, as the sun dipped below the horizon, painting the sky with hues of orange and purple, Bodhi called all the creatures of the forest to gather. Beneath the shimmering canopy of leaves,

a clearing emerged, bathed in the warm glow of fireflies. This was the stage where the grand dance of existence would unfold, and Bodhi, with its wrinkled bark and knowing gaze, would be the silent observer.

First to appear were the thoughts, flitting like playful butterflies, leaving trails of memories and dreams that shimmered like stardust. Each thought danced a unique pattern, weaving together a tapestry of the forest's collective consciousness. Bodhi watched in awe as the thoughts intertwined, creating a beautiful mosaic of the forest's inner world.

Next, swirling into the clearing, came the feelings. Joy danced with reckless abandon, while Sorrow followed close behind, their contrasting movements adding depth and richness to the dance.

Each emotion, vibrant and alive, contributed to the ever-shifting emotional landscape of the forest.

From the earth, sensations arose, grounding the dance with their rhythmic energy. The gentle rustling of leaves, the warmth of sunlight on fur, and the cool touch of the breeze on skin - each sensation played its part, resonating through the clearing, making the forest come alive.

Then, perceptions joined the dance, adding color and depth to the experience.

Sight, a captivating dancer adorned with the colors of the rainbow, painted vibrant scenes onto the canvas of awareness. Sound, a gifted musician, played the melodies of chirping birds and rustling leaves, creating a symphony that filled the air.

And lastly, taste and smell, the mystical duo, entered the fray. The air was filled with the sweet fragrance of blooming flowers and the earthy scent of the forest floor, while the taste of fresh air awakened the senses of the forest creatures.

With each movement, with each sound and sensation, the forest dance grew. It became a vibrant tapestry woven from the threads of thoughts, feelings, sensations, and perceptions, all guided by the unseen hand of awareness.

Bodhi, the ancient witness, spoke to the creatures of the forest, its voice a gentle whisper carried on the wind. "Little ones," it said, "you are all dancers in this grand performance. Your movements, your expressions, your very presence contribute to the beauty of this dance. And just as the ripples on a pond eventually fade away, so too do your thoughts, feelings, and sensations come and go, leaving behind the vastness of awareness, a constant presence that holds everything within its embrace."

A hush fell over the enchanted clearing. The creatures stood still, their gazes fixed on Bodhi, their hearts filled with newfound understanding. They realized that they were not just participants in the dance, but also the dance itself.

They were the thoughts, the feelings, the sensations, and the perceptions, all arising and dissolving within the vast ocean of awareness. And so, the dance continued, now with a deeper meaning. The forest had awakened to its true nature, a place where the timeless rhythm of existence resonated in every leaf, every creature, every thought, feeling, sensation, and perception. And Bodhi, the gentle giant, stood tall, a silent guardian of this magical symphony that played on in the heart of the enchanted forest.

9.1 Guided Meditation

1. Find a quiet space and sit or lie down comfortably. Close your eyes and take a few deep breaths, inhaling slowly through your nose and exhaling through your mouth.

2. Imagine yourself in a magical forest bathed in soft, golden light. Feel the ground beneath you, connecting with the earth's energy.

3. Envision Bodhi, the wise old tree, standing tall in the center of the forest. Its branches reach out, and its leaves rustle gently in the breeze.

4. Become aware of your thoughts as playful butterflies, dancing and leaving trails of stardust. Observe each thought with curiosity, letting them flit by without attachment.

5. Feel the emotions entering the clearing, each emotion dancing with its own unique rhythm. Allow joy, sorrow, and other feelings to move through you, acknowledging their presence.

6. Ground yourself with sensations, sensing the rustling leaves, the warmth of sunlight, and the cool breeze on your skin. Feel the rhythm of the forest energy flowing through you.

7. Let your perceptions join the dance. Imagine vibrant scenes painted by Sight and melodies played by Sound, adding color and depth to your awareness.

8. Embrace the mystical duo of Taste and Smell. Inhale the sweet fragrance of blooming flowers and the earthy scent of the forest floor. Taste the freshness of the air.

9. Recognize that you are part of this grand dance, contributing to the beauty of the forest's symphony. Your thoughts, feelings, sensations, and perceptions are the threads weaving a vibrant tapestry of awareness.

10. Listen to Bodhi's gentle whisper on the wind, acknowledging the impermanence of your experiences. Realize that, like ripples on a pond, your thoughts and feelings come and go, but awareness remains constant.

11. Take a few more deep breaths, gradually bringing your awareness back to the present moment. Open your eyes when you feel ready, carrying the sense of awareness with you.

To access additional meditations
and resources, scan the QR code

9.2 (A) Worksheet

(A) Draw Your Forest Dance:

Use colored pencils or markers to draw a forest scene. Represent your thoughts, feelings, sensations, and perceptions as various elements in the dance. Get creative!

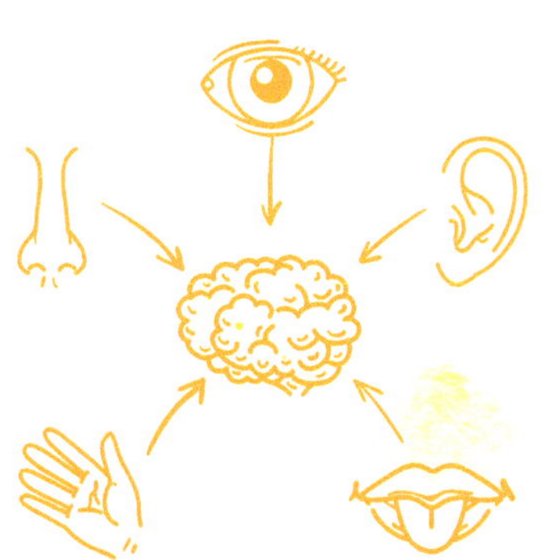

9.2 (B) Worksheet

(B) Thought Butterflies:

Below are the butterflies, each representing a different thought. Write the nature of the thought beside each butterfly. Are they playful, curious, or fleeting?

9.2 (C) Worksheet

(C) Awareness Mandala

In the center of your drawing, create a mandala symbolizing awareness. Use patterns, shapes, and colors to represent the constant presence that holds everything together.

9.2 (D) Worksheet

(D) Reflection:

Write a short paragraph reflecting on your experience. How did the guided meditation help you understand the dance of awareness in your own life? How can you carry this awareness into your daily activities?